SOCIAL LIVES OF
LIONS

ANIMAL BEHAVIORS

Elliot Riley

Rourke
Educational Media

rourkeeducationalmedia.com

Scan for Related Titles
and Teacher Resources

Teaching Focus:

Vocabulary: Continue to provide direct vocabulary instruction as well as instruction to help students learn how to infer the meanings of words they encounter when they are reading.

Before Reading:

Building Academic Vocabulary and Background Knowledge

Before reading a book, it is important to set the stage for your child or student by using pre-reading strategies. This will help them develop their vocabulary, increase their reading comprehension, and make connections across the curriculum.

1. Read the title and look at the cover. *Let's make predictions about what this book will be about.*
2. Take a picture walk by talking about the pictures/photographs in the book. Implant the vocabulary as you take the picture walk. Be sure to talk about the text features such as headings, Table of Contents, glossary, bolded words, captions, charts/diagrams, and Index.
3. Have students read the first page of text with you then have students read the remaining text.
4. Strategy Talk – use to assist students while reading.
   - Get your mouth ready
   - Look at the picture
   - Think…does it make sense
   - Think…does it look right
   - Think…does it sound right
   - Chunk it – by looking for a part you know
5. Read it again.
6. After reading the book complete the activities below.

Content Area Vocabulary
Use glossary words in a sentence.

complex
dominant
familiar
hierarchy
intensity
nurse

After Reading:

Comprehension and Extension Activity

After reading the book, work on the following questions with your child or students in order to check their level of reading comprehension and content mastery.

1. *What does it mean when male lions in a pride rub their heads together?* (Summarize)
2. *What is a group of lions called?* (Asking questions)
3. *How long do lion cubs stay with their mothers?* (Text to self connection)
4. *After reading the book, what can you summarize about lions?* (Summarize)

Extension Activity

Now that you have read about lions, how about making your own lion mask? You will need a paper plate, scissors, yellow construction paper, brown yarn, glue and a popsicle stick. Cute a round circle the size of the paper plate from the yellow construction paper. Glue it to the paper plate. Also, cut out two ears and glue them to the top of the plate. Cut two holes for you eyes. Cut strips of the brown yarn and glue them on the mask as the mane and whiskers. Glue the popsicle stick to the bottom of the plate. Now hold it up to your face. Look in the mirror. Do you look like a lion? Now, make some loud, growling sounds!

Table of Contents

Social Cats

Have you ever seen lions rub their heads together? Did you wonder why?

Lions are the only cat species in the world that form social groups. These groups are called prides.

Prides may include up to three males, about a dozen females, and their cubs.

Females usually stay in their mother's pride for life. Young males are forced out when they are large enough to compete with the **dominant** males.

female lion (lioness)

male lion

young male lion

Lion Language

Lions need to have many ways to communicate with each other.

Lions talk to each other using various calls. Each call may have a different volume, tone, and **intensity**. Their calls include snarls, moans, roars, grunts, growls, meows, purrs, and hums.

Lions also use body language to communicate. Male lions in the same pride will greet each other by rubbing their heads together.

Male lions that are not part of a pride will try to take over by attacking the pride's males. When male lions in a pride rub their heads together, they're saying, "When the time comes to fight, I've got your back!"

Female lions lick and nuzzle the other females in the pride. Females will also rub their heads against the males in the pride.

Lions seem to have the most **complex** communication behaviors of all the big cats.

These behaviors are thought to strengthen the social bonds or attachment between the pride members. If a lion does not greet others this way, this signals it is not part of the pride.

Protective and Playful

A lioness is fiercely protective of her cubs. Young lions are dependent on their mothers for up to two years. Lionesses will **nurse** the cubs of other close relatives in the pride, as long as they are younger than her own.

Female lions often give birth at about the same time, so the cubs within a pride are close in age.

When a new male lion takes over a pride, he will try to kill all the cubs in the pride. Protecting their cubs from these lions is one reason lionesses live in groups.

The members of a pride take care of each other. The lionesses hunt for food together, while the males offer protection from other lions.

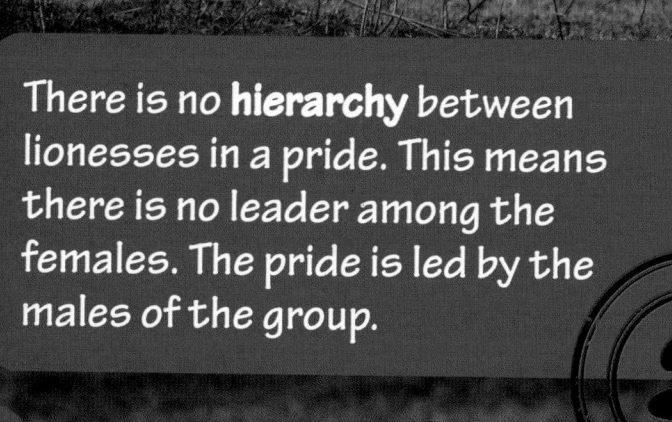

There is no **hierarchy** between lionesses in a pride. This means there is no leader among the females. The pride is led by the males of the group.

Lion cubs like to play. They pounce, wrestle, and run. Sometimes they like to play with their mother's tail!

Playtime is important for lion cubs. It helps them develop bonds with the other cubs and adults in the pride.

Play is also a chance to practice the skills they will need as adults. Stalking, pouncing, and play fighting help cubs develop these abilities.

Lionesses tend to remain playful as adults. Male lions do not. If a male adult plays with a cub, the cub's mother will keep a close eye on them to make sure it doesn't get too rough.

Unusual Bonds

Sometimes a lion or an entire pride will accept, or bond with, a human. These lions may have been rescued, or saved, by the person.

The lions recognize the person and treat them as a member of the pride. They use greeting behaviors that indicate they are **familiar** with each other.

Lions are also known to bond with other species. Lionesses in the wild have adopted baby antelopes, oryxes, and baboons.

In *one case*, a rescued lion, tiger, and bear became best friends.

Photo Glossary

complex (KAHM-pleks): When something is complex, it has multiple elements that make it complicated, rather than simple.

dominant (DA-muh-nuhnt): Someone or something that is dominant exerts the most power or influence in a group.

familiar (fuh-MIL-yur): Something or someone you know well is familiar to you. They are recognizable.

hierarchy (HYE-ur-ahr-kee): A hierarchy is an arrangement in a group in which people or animals have different ranks or levels of importance.

intensity (in-TENTS-uh-tee): Intensity indicates force or strength. A roar with lower intensity has a different meaning than one with higher intensity.

nurse (nurs): To nurse a baby means to feed it with milk from a teat or breast.

Index

Websites to Visit

www.animalfactguide.com/animal-facts/lion
http://kids.nationalgeographic.com/
    animals/lion
http://kids.sandiegozoo.org/animals/
    mammals/african-lion

Meet The Author!
www.meetREMauthors.cor

About the Author

Elliot Riley is an author and animal lover in Tampa, Florida. When she's not writing or watching animal videos, you can find her reading in her favorite hammock or hanging out with her four kids.

Edited by: Keli Sipperley
Cover design, interior design and art direction: Nicola Stratford
www.nicolastratford.com

Library of Congress PCN Data

Social Lives of Lions / Elliot Riley
(Animal Behaviors)
ISBN 978-1-68191-699-6 (hard cover)
ISBN 978-1-68191-800-6 (soft cover)
ISBN 978-1-68191-897-6 (e-Book)
Library of Congress Control Number: 2016932575

Rourke Educational Media
Printed in the United States of America, North Mankato, Minnesota

www.rourkeeducationalmedia.com

PHOTO CREDITS: Cover © Yongyut Kunsri (Savannah), Ecliptic Blue (lion & cub); Page 4 © Maggy Meyer, Page 5 © Stuart G Porter; Page 6 © Sergei Domashenko, Page 7 © Maggy Meyer; Page 8 © Lara Zanarini, Page 9 © JacoBecker; Page 10 © Villiers Steyn, Page 11 © Maggy Meyer; Page 12 © Edwin Butter, Page 13 © GUDKOV ANDREY; Page 14 © Kjetil Kolbjornsrud, Page 15 © JONATHAN PLEDGER; Page 16 © AndreAnita, Page 17 © Ana Gram; Page 18 © Nick Biemans, Page 19 © meunierd; Page 20 © Nolte Lourens, Page 21 © apple2499; Page 23 (bottom picture) © zagart116
All photos from Shutterstock.com

Also Available as:

24